The
Relunctant
Medium

by
Susan Sanderford
and
Dr. Coleen Allen

Published by: Spirit Wind Ink
                  Susan & Milt Sanderford
                  P.O. Box 64
                  San Luis, Colorado 81152
                  iheart2@mac.com

Cover Art "Sacred Geometry 240" by Endre Balogh
www.EndresArt.com

To order additional copies of this book please visit:
www.amazon.com

ISBN-10: 1985729873
ISBN-13: 978-1985729872

Printed in USA – 2018

Contents

Forward   v

Introduction   vii

The Reluctant Medium

In the Beginning Was the Word ...

And the Word Was—Depression!   1

Ask and You Shall Receive   7

God Speaks   11

Where He Leads Me, Will I Follow?   15

Talk About the "Far Side!"   25

OK God – PROVE IT!   31

Welcome Back Little Child

Colene Allen's Story   35

Believe or not to believe

Was that the question?   41

To Make a Point   45

The Reunion   53

The Release   61

Farewell but not goodbye   67

Face to face with an old friend   71

Welcome back little child   75

The Ripple Effect   79

Proof received and acknowledged   87

Forward

On April 11, 2004, world-famous medium James Van Praagh had listed on his website at www.vanpraagh.com, ten mediums from around the world he felt merited his personal recommendation as reputable. On April 12th James added recommended medium number eleven—Susan K. Sanderford. At that time, Susan was also listed on James' site as one of three recommended authentic spiritual teachers.

This all came about when Susan reunited one of her grief counseling clients with her precious son who had committed suicide a year prior. While in James' chat room, the woman mentioned the "miraculous" reading she received from Susan.

His interest piqued, James contacted Susan asking for a reading for himself in order to experience Susan's gift. (An audition so to speak!) Several weeks after his session James asked Susan to do a session for a close friend.

That accomplished, several weeks later James asked for one more reading for another close friend.

Needless to say, the sessions were beyond their expectations and so reported to James, leading to his recommendation as Susan qualifying as a reputable medium.

Her name is Susan K. Sanderford and she is a spiritual medium who communicates with deceased loved ones and spirit guides. When this mediumship phenomenon first surfaced, she did not seek this ability, didn't want this ability, in fact she fought it all the way.

You see, Susan was raised in the church as a fundamentalist Christian where mediumship, communicating with the dead, was considered anti-Christian. With so many negative church rules already hanging over her head—she certainly didn't need another.

Deciding that God According to Man had not served her well, she asked God to show her what His truth was. It was at that moment she asked God to be her teacher. To her amazement, God showed up!

This is Susan's story. The Reluctant Medium.

Introduction

*"For those who believe—
no proof is necessary.
For those who do not believe—
no proof is possible."*

We do not travel this earth-life alone!

Each of us have spirit guides, loved ones and assigned helpers who assist us through difficult times. It's their job. I know this —because they have told me so.

My name is Susan Sanderford. I'm a spiritual medium—and I communicate with those now living in the spirit dimension. (Some call it heaven or "The Other Side.") The spirit dimension is where we all began and is where we will all eventually return to continue our eternal existence.

Over the past twenty-one years I have engaged in over 10,000 conversations with those entities living in the spirit dimension. My goal is to share their stories and current activities in an attempt to bring those on planet earth, who are interested, into awareness and enlightenment.

Susan Sanderford

Chapter One

In the Beginning Was the Word ...
And the Word Was—Depression!

"GOD, WHERE ARE YOU?" was the soulful cry from the depths of an aching heart. At age 37 I felt my life to be an empty and miserable existence. Something was so very wrong, but I was powerless to determine what.

From that sorry abyss came my plea, "God, I've been doing it right all these years, believing and practicing what I had been taught, following the rules, attending church, praying, reading my Bible, witnessing, attending Bible College." Yet something of major significance was missing.

The answer jolted my being. The missing piece to complete the puzzle was—God! Where was God? How could this be? Growing up in a Christian home, church and God seemed our family's way of life. Attending every service our church had to offer, we were taught and believed doctrine that separated us from other forms of religion, taking pride in the fact that we worshipped God closest to the way the disciples did in the Old Testament. Our leaders in the church implied we had the corner on the market of true worship as the Bible instructed, and we were the ones that had "The Truth."

In Sunday School, we were taught that Christ died for our sins and that to enter Heaven we must put our trust and faith in Jesus Christ alone. Jesus was the only way and if we didn't believe in Christ we would go to a place called hell, a miserable fiery den where Satan and his angels would anguish with us throughout eternity. Now that scared me!

At summer church camp I asked Jesus to come into my heart. I was ten years old and knew I didn't want to go to hell. It was evening story time where I was told I was a worthless miserable sinner in need of being saved and that Jesus died for my sins to save me from hell. It seemed the right decision was to accept His death on my behalf, the option being what it was.

It's doubtful the message of Jesus' death and resurrection was truly grasped, for there seemed to be no power in my life that allowed me to walk as a child of God, no matter how hard I tried.

Fear and guilt still hounded me after that salvation experience. Where were the miracles? Was I not doing something, right? Believing in Jesus Christ dying for my sins was all there was to being a Christian—so I was told. Now entrance to heaven was assured and all I had to do was to obey the rules, because this is what Christians do. On the other hand, expect God's punishment if you failed to measure up to those rules. If not immediately, somehow, some time, you will pay the consequences of any misdeeds.

This teaching caused me to believe that God was not a very forgiving being, and rather big on payback.

Drilled into my mind throughout those tender years as a Christian, I needed to obey the Bible (God's Word) because that was the only way I could come to know God.

My charted course was clear—to do and be the very best because this was what my church, family, and God expected of me. Blindly following what everyone else around me believed, fear was always a part of the equation. After all, in order for God, church and family to love me, I had to do and be what they wanted.

Always hanging over my head was the intimidating thought, "I better not make a wrong step else God's Almighty wrath will surely strike me down." Had my teachers never heard of, or experienced Unconditional Love? Sadly, it took me 38 years to discover that God loved me just as I was—unconditionally.

In His eyes, I was worthy without doing or being anything. He totally loved and accepted me as I was, and worked on molding me at that point. It took me 38 years to understand that is how God wants us to love each other— our children, friends, and even strangers. My religion had it backwards!

I had relied on church and family to guide me correctly, yet on this 23rd day of October in 1993 I was totally miserable. Now slumped on my sofa, mother of three fine boys, a dejected and disillusioned wife and Christian—I called out to God in all my pain and futility, "GOD! Something must be wrong with the way I'm doing this Christian thing because I don't see You God, I don't feel You."

"Where are You? Where is that powerful God that parted the Red Sea? Where is the God of miracles? THERE MUST BE ANOTHER WAY because this one is not working, I'm miserable, lonely and empty. God, I feel like

I'm at my wits end." I literally felt weeping from the core of my soul.

"That's it!!! I'm throwing everything I've learned out the window and I want You to teach me Truth God, because what I've been taught by man about Your Truth is empty and powerless. Teach me Your Truth God and I'll do anything you want me to do in service to You!" That's all it took. That simple request in heart-felt sincerity set God into motion, working in my life in ways I never thought God would or could.

I felt no release from my misery at that instant nor were my problems washed away by a blinding miracle. Importantly though, it was the beginning, the first step. After all these years, this was when I finally began to discover God. To my surprise—He wasn't where I thought He would be.

Chapter Two

Ask and Ye Shall Receive

"But the Helper, the Holy Spirit, whom the Father will send in My name, He will teach you all things, and bring to your remembrance all that I said to you."—Jesus

John 14:26

Here's a guarantee for you. When you cry out in sincerity for God to help, God always answers—often not in the timing or ways we expect, or would prefer, but always with an answer that is for our highest good and for the highest good of everyone involved. When we invite God into our lives His transforming work strikes at the very center of our belief system—both in our hearts and in our minds. Thankfully, truth is not usually rained upon us in one tremendous storm, rather is often revealed as one gentle spring shower followed by another—as we are ready to absorb it. If truth were dumped in our laps all in one fell swoop, we would likely not accept it as truth, but reject it as too radical and not applicable.

Isn't that what was done with Jesus two thousand years ago. He was the embodiment of Truth. People feared this man and the Truth He represented. Most chose not to see the Truth sent from God, but rather rejected His teachings and crucified Him.

As each of us searches for truth, God takes us where we are and as we are, and begins to transform our thinking, renewing our minds from that point forward. Very gently He begins to undo our wrong thinking.

Whether Catholic, Methodist, Presbyterian, Fundamentalist Christian, Buddhist, Muslim, or Agnostic, God begins at the very point where we ask for His help. Because He is God, therefore unlimited, He takes our existing framework and begins to remove thoughts, beliefs and perceptions that are in error, replacing them with His Truth—but always within the framework of our current belief system. Before long we learn that most of the old beliefs we held so tightly have no value at all in the eyes of God. We learn they have served to give us a false sense of security. This is not to say the forms of religion in the world today are not important to our spiritual awakening. But when we worship religion as the only way that leads us to God then we have missed the point. We have created idols out of our religions rather than finding our way back to God through them.

Once we make the decision to truly find and know God, our spiritual evolution begins. If we continue on that path without slipping back into our old beliefs and fears, the time of transformation can be relatively short. However, because of our free will to make choices we often delay the process by many years when we choose not to listen and follow the Truth God is revealing to us. That choice is up to us.

Healing, cleansing and miracle after miracle took place in my life after that day I cried out to God to teach me, remake me and use me as He saw fit. Mind boggling, eye opening, spirit freeing miracles—all involving the mystical and metaphysical.

Chapter Three

God Speaks

After this invitation to God to teach me truth and due to circumstances beyond my control, I found myself being thrust into the newspaper publishing business. Notwithstanding, my prior newspaper graphics experience, there's no way I wanted to be publishing a monthly newspaper, especially on my very own, yet that seemed to be the direction God was leading.

I will never forget the first time I heard The Voice. "Do not be afraid, I will be with you!" I twirled around to see who was in the back seat of the car. Massive chills ran down my spine, no one was there.

My tears had flowed for two days. Buying this business was going against all that I believed God wanted for me. "How do I know it's You God" I cried while driving home from Bible study that evening. At that desperate moment of overwhelming fear The Voice commanded once again, "Do not be afraid, I will be with you!" Instantly the fear was released and a wonderful feeling of peace coursed through me. I knew this was God. I answered, "OK, God, I don't understand it, and most certainly don't like it, but if this is what you want, I'll accept it." You see, I asked God for help, listened for His answer, and decided to follow this directive, even though it went against what I thought was right.

The endless flow of tears of the past few days dramatically ceased with those comforting words. That peace that passes all understanding enveloped my total being and flowed through me. At that moment, the realization struck—I could move ahead without fear. God was with me. He just told me so!

The next morning in my devotions I read the story of Peter getting out of the boat in the midst of a storm. Peter said the exact words to Jesus as I had said to God the night before. "How do I know it's You!" And Jesus reached out his hand and said "Come!" Peter stepped out of the boat and walked on water to reach Jesus. I knew at that moment those words were for me. I had to step out of the boat and trust God that this was the direction my life was to take. "Come, Susan, I will be with you."

Growing up in the church I had been taught that God only spoke to prophets and apostles. You had to be a chosen vessel of God to hear God's voice. I was also taught that the Bible was the only way that He spoke to us in these modern days, yet God had spoken to me just last evening.

It was this experience that began my questioning of my early teaching, the beliefs upon which my very foundation was built. God was beginning to replace my illusions with His Truth.

Chapter Four

Where He Leads Me, Will I Follow?

In the midst of my spiritual searching, God brought Milt Sanderford into my life. This new-found business associate and soon to be best friend, proved literally to be a God-send.

My second recognized exposure to the metaphysical occurred four months after Milt and I met. It was in the form of a dream in November of 1994. Having mentioned my departed grandfather to Milt one morning at work, that very night, for the first time ever, I dreamt of my grandfather. A dream so vivid I felt it was real.

In the dream my grandfather was letting me know that he was doing well and was indeed happy in his present surroundings. He was radiant, with a brilliant white light shining from him. The next day at work describing the dream to Milt, his response opened my mind to a world beyond that which we see around us.

"Was it just a dream, or was your grandfather actually communicating with you?"

To understand the impact his question carried, one needs to be aware of Milt's "being". Although we had just become business associates some four months prior, we quickly grew to be best friends, in fact, the best friend I've ever had in all my life.

The friendship was built upon a mutual liking, accepting, respecting and caring. There were no flirtations or attempts to inject romantic activities into this beautiful friendship. Over the months, I realized how unique and special this man was. I never knew anyone so happy and giving—not just to me, but to all he met. For the first time in my entire life, I actually saw God in a fellow human being.

Now Milt and I were speaking comfortably on a subject neither had broached to this point in our friendship. He went on to share a warm and loving experience of communicating with his wife who had passed away in 1981. Several days after Mary Jane died, Milt (also, a skeptical fundamentalist at the time) was told he would be led to a trance medium within thirty-days, one who would put him in touch with his beloved wife. It happened. The trance medium's name was Hester B. Jackson, a Virginia Beach resident. Milt and Hester's close friendship ended with her death in 1983.

Hearing his story of reunion with Mary Jane from beyond the grave, and his developed friendship with Hester, I began to seriously consider the possibility of spirit contact. After the contact from my grandfather, I began sending thoughts to my grandmother, asking where she was and what she was doing since passing on. I knew my grandfather had a "salvation experience," but did not know that to be true of her. (I suspected if any of our family would wind up in hell it would be my grandmother.)

Within two weeks she visited me in a dream, explaining what she was now doing in such a way that left no doubt that those words were not my subconscious playing tricks. My grandmother was communicating with me from the beyond.

In early January 1995, I experienced another dream, so vivid, each detail is permanently etched in my memory. The first "full-color" dream I ever dreamt. It was precognitive, foretelling a monumental event about to take place in my life—a true burning-bush experience of Biblical proportions. The events in the dream became a reality within two weeks, and it was then I started asking "How could this possibly not be from God?"

The dream was very symbolic in its meaning and revealed that my bound spirit was about to be set free through Love. Because of my faithfulness and surrender to His will, God allowed me to experience true Godly Love for the first time in my life. At 38, I realized I had never given or received true unconditional Love, nor did I even understand what Love was until I discovered its presence between Milt and me in a very dramatic way.

The Christmas and New Year holidays passed, and we were back to work readying the February "Love Issue" of our newspaper, The Mirror. As was our custom, Milt and I left the office for breakfast at Courtney's in Winter Park, Florida. I was feeling emotionally down-and-out. The holidays had been particularly miserable for me. I felt lost and empty.

Toward the end of our meal I shared my sadness with Milt by revealing my sense that never in my life had anyone loved me—for just being me! There always seemed to be conditions. I had to act a certain way, be a certain way, believe a certain way, do certain things—but never loving me because I was—

me! Tears welled in my eyes and heart.

In his loving brotherly way, Milt reached over and placed my hand in his, looked into my soul and said, "Susan, I love you just the way you are, and I always will!" I believed him, and it felt so wonderful. Without pause, I then went on to reveal what I believe was one of the most important statements of my life. "Milt, when you were on vacation over the holidays, it dawned on me that it was the first time in my entire life I actually missed someone—ever!"

As soon as the words left my mouth, it was like a giant hand reached down and tore a blindfold from my eyes. A revelation of great truth. I couldn't breathe, as though I had just received a tremendous blow to the stomach. "My God." I thought, "This is what love is!" I couldn't speak.

I prayed that when I stood my legs would do their job of getting me out of the restaurant, to the car, and back home as quickly as possible. I was in a state of shock. As we returned to the office I was able to say no more than a goodbye to Milt, followed by an awkward bear hug that caused him to fall back into his chair.

Once home I opened my Bible to the "Love" chapter, II Corinthians, Chapter 13. Love is very patient and kind, never jealous or envious, never boastful or proud, never haughty or selfish or rude. Love does not demand its own way. It is not irritable or touchy. It does not hold grudges and will hardly ever notice when others do it wrong. Without Love, you are nothing!

I spoke aloud, "God, this is it. Now I see. You brought Milt into my life to show me what love is. I have been faithful to You, and You now reward Your willing servant! Thank you, God!" That night as I was driving my son Mathew to a Wheel of Fortune tryout at Disney World, I reached over and touched him. It felt so good. It was the first time in my life I was able to touch someone from a place of Love! My life had been changed forever, A miracle! The very next day I went to work and confidently informed Milt that he was in love with me! "God brought you into my life to show me what true love is!" His sweet and tender voice whispered "I know!" (Our love story is worthy of a book in itself).

It was truly a burning-bush experience. A deeply spiritual and wonderfully explosive passionate Love that only God's blessing and presence can create between two people. I saw God in Milt, now I saw and experienced God's Love in myself. What a life-changing revelation.

Being 24 years older than me, and realizing he would likely precede me in death, I began to read books on the subject thinking it would be wonderful to communicate with Milt after he passed on. With his considerable writing talent, I felt perhaps he would be able to write books through me, enabling us to share the closeness we developed on this earth. (His running joke was "I can hardly wait!") There's no question my interest was for a selfish purpose, but I quickly learned that God had other reasons for me to develop this gift.

In my research, particularly impressive was the book Milt shared with me, There is a River, by Thomas Sugrue, the story of Edgar Cayce, well-known Christian psychic who throughout his exemplary life was able to put his mind in contact with universal information through a self-induced sleep. When asked questions while in this trance-like sleep, he produced valuable insights on everything from maintaining a well-balanced diet and improving human relationships to overcoming life-threatening illnesses, how to treat various maladies and experiencing a closer walk with God.

Obviously not for financial gain or fame, here was a man who spent his entire life serving others with his God given gifts. We are told, "By their fruits ye shall know them". For me, Edgar Cayce's life validated the legitimacy of that vast world beyond our human senses.

After reading his well-documented life story I began to accept that God can and does work in different and mysterious ways. Through these books, and the encouragement of others, I added meditation to my morning prayer and Bible reading.

After reading a book by Ruth Montgomery, a former newswoman who channeled spirits through automatic writing, among them famed American psychic Arthur Ford, I sat at the computer keyboard to meditate and decided to give it a try. I began writing the impressions that came into my mind and was immediately overwhelmed at the clarity of the information coming to me.

Not trusting the information was being supplied other than by my own overactive imagination, I asked for a validation that it was indeed coming from spirit. The answer I received was an eye-opener! Now as you read this, how many of you are aware of the exact number of food cans sitting in your pantry? I was told to go and count those in mine, and that I would find twelve.

Astounded, I raced back to the computer keyboard and typed "You are right. Give me another validation!" Patiently, and I must say, with an interesting sense of humor, my guest spirit communicator said "You have 32 bath towels in the house! Go count them!" Picture this searcher-for-the-truth, not quite certain if her mind had been lost forever, dashing madly through the house, tearing through closets, drawers and hampers, until the magic number had been located.

I was absolutely amazed, and thus began my introduction to spirit communication. Sharing the experience with Milt that evening in our nightly good-night call, he suggested I ask the name of my new-found friend.

"By what name do I call you?" I asked. To my absolute astonishment, glee and delight, my new-found spirit pen-pal introduced herself as Hester B. Jackson, Milt's good friend who died in 1983. Hester informed me she was now officially in charge of my mediumship development.

"Because of your seeking heart, humbleness, and surrender, you have been chosen by God to serve Him in this way!" she informed. Even though I believed I was communicating with spirit, I continued to be skeptical as to the possible spiritual value of such activity. Taking seriously the admonition to seek, search and knock, I sought truth by way of prayer, Bible study and meditation. If this was of God, I asked Him to leave not a shred of doubt in my mind.

Chapter Five

Talk About the "Far Side!"

There were times I actually thought I was going crazy, having slipped on the edge of the cliff dropping into the depths of madness. Spirits were now talking to me day and night, at home and in my car. Spirits cheering me on—congratulating my awakening and encouraging me to press forward.

It was like a dam being opened, with deceased friends and relatives of Milt's flowing through, proclaiming their wish to work with or just encourage me in my psychic training. It was at this time that Hester informed me that Milt was a master teacher having no need to return to earth, but he made the choice to come back to serve as an earthly guide to help me and several others with their spiritual development, it was so overwhelming.

There was Milt's father, Dad Alcorn who shared he had always silently admired Milt's spirituality, and Milt's former wife Mary Jane who told me she remains nearby as a symbol of love "Because he saved my soul!" Milt's spirit guide, fun-loving Chief Laughing Water shared that Milt had been a great chief in a prior life, and was looking forward to working with him again. With their similar off-the-wall sense of humor, they seemed to be the perfect match.

Hester described her function as one who chose to help me with the mechanics of developing my mediumship, acting as my chief trainer, guide, cheerleader and gatekeeper to spirit communication. What a kind and loving spirit, soon to become a good friend, taskmaster and supporter.

Hester made it clear that the development of my spirituality and understanding of God's Truths would be in the hands of the Holy Spirit, the teacher God has promised to us all. These events were all so exciting and revolutionary to my mind and my senses, yet I was still troubled. Talk about your mixed emotions! Picture this if you will!

This was all happening to one who was raised as a Fundamentalist Christian. If there was any doubt before, there was little question now that I was headed straight to hell on the fast-track. Was this God's idea of a joke? If so, I wasn't laughing. Why me?

I was overtaken by visions of a darkly lit room

with a beaded doorway leading to a heavy-set, hard-looking, make-up-laden woman seated at a table gazing into a crystal ball while asking someone to cross her palm with silver. These impressions crowded and clouded my mind. How could this be? God, why do I have this ability? Where did it come from? I thought this kind of thing was evil?

Is this really what happens to someone who surrenders to You? These questions and more exploded into my mind when I truly realized I was developing abilities far beyond those most people consider normal. In the beginning, it was difficult to accept that I could communicate with souls who had departed their physical bodies. It felt as though something had grabbed me by the neck and dragged me kicking and screaming into this strange metaphysical new-age stuff. In fact, I left heel marks on the floor and fingernail scratches in the wall every inch of the way. When I cried out "God, I'll serve you any way you want, I'll do whatever you ask of me!"—I certainly didn't mean this.

What had I done to open this flood-gate into the world of the metaphysical? I most certainly was not prepared to accept the responsibility. "God, I don't want this, I liked it the way it was. Simple to understand rules—even though they were man's rules." I had not studied nor even believed in anything metaphysical. I was raised in a "Christian" environment and was lead to believe that anything of this nature was of Satan.

What caused this turn-around in my life? The only thing I could attribute it to was that I had surrendered my life—one-hundred percent of it, to God. It didn't take long to realize it was God's hand on the back of my neck, gently guiding me kicking and screaming into this new reality. And now God was asking me to share my story?

To encourage, Hester shared the following;

Discouragement is easy when you focus on negative things. Try always to focus on the positive. Make a list of things that are good in your life, and focus on those things. You must create the world around you as you want it to be, with love, joy, peace, patience, gentleness, kindness and self-control. The fruits of the Spirit are there for your asking, but you must first ask with a sincere heart.

Fruit will be produced when you are ready to accept your calling. Fruit and growth is always dependent upon your willingness to let go and allow God to do His work in you. You cannot produce the fruit. Only God. Relax and enjoy all that is yours, even if you do not have it yet. Do not be afraid to let go of anything that binds you to this earth, for in the letting go you will find Life.

Keep looking to God even when you do not sense His presence. He is always there, beside you and in you. He is ready to do His work to clear your mind of control and your desires. I know this is a difficult time adjusting to your new life and abilities. This will soon pass as you become more accustomed to our presence and purpose.

Blessings will come soon, do not worry. This is just a time of preparation for you. It is a time of getting ready for battle. For the fight will not be easy, but will be very rewarding. There will come a time when all of this will be as second nature to you and you will love and enjoy the excitement of seeing others move toward God. We cannot tell you much right now as these things are to be learned as life is played out. Just trust and have faith in God that He does not let any of His sheep go astray. He will come back and gather them in His arms and bring them back to His fold to protect, Love and care for. You are one of His Sheep. Always look to the Shepherd for Guidance.

Listen to Milt, he knows these things. You are so fortunate to have him as an earthly teacher and guide. He will be your visible strength. Continue to meditate, breathe and practice what we share with you. All these things will become organized for you soon, and you will understand how all work together. All will soon become clear Trust in God, He is your Hope.

I am so pleased to be working with you. There are so few Godly channels to work through. It's a great accomplishment to find one. Much can be done through one such as you. You will become a leader in this field. You have been chosen because of your humble and pure intent to serve God. You are blessed. You are as a daughter to me.

I love you.

Hester

Emotionally moved, I responded, "I love you too Hester, and I'll try my best to follow God's path for me!"

At this point I could certainly identify with Saul of Tarsus when he met God on the Road to Damascus. He was knocked off his horse and got up a changed man. Well, I also got knocked off my "fundamental high-horse" and got up a changed woman.

Lord, give me strength!

Chapter Six

OK God – PROVE IT!

Despite Hester's and Milt's encouragement to continue in my mediumship development, my early beliefs as a Fundamentalist Christian still paralyzed my mind with fear. I needed some kind of definitive proof that this road I was being asked to take would somehow serve God and his children. Where could that proof be found other than through God alone? Thus, my challenge to Him!

"OK God, if this is the path you want me to follow, show me how it will serve your purpose, and please, make it abundantly clear!" Surprisingly it didn't take long.

Up to this point the only person I did "readings" for was Milt. They were in two forms. I shared messages for him that I received from his loved ones in spirit, his dad Ed Alcorn, his wife Mary Jane, guides like Hester and Chief Laughing Water.

In his insistence to "prove" the accuracy of information I was receiving, Milt also devised his own "proof validation process!" His feeling was, if this was to be a part of our future, we better make certain it's an honest and legitimate path we're taking. Through just his thought process, Milt would ask a question of spirit, and without sharing with me, he would then ask me "OK, what do you get now?"

I would then clear my mind and focus on the thoughts that would enter my being, then I'd share them with Milt exactly as received, all the while the tape recorder picked up my responses. We'd do this for about an hour each session, Milt sitting on a chair with his notepad and me lying on the bed with my eyes covered. Not that there was anything I could peek at, but it was more relaxing for me. After the session, Milt would share with me the subject matter of his questions to spirit, and we'd replay spirit's responses as given to me – again, all through the thought process. Telepathy in its simplest form.

The subjects Milt came up with ranged from Marilyn Monroe and President Kennedy to baseball players from the past and old movies. One particular question and spirit's response that deeply touched Milt concerned a favorite baseball player from Milt's youth. He asked spirit – again, silently through his thought process, "What can you tell me about Andy that I don't already know?"

When he asked me, "OK, what do you get?" I paused and shared, "What they are showing me is a man in a wheel chair. It looks like he has no legs and someone is pushing him down a hallway. That's all I am being shown."

The following day when Milt did an internet search on the player he was astounded and saddened to learn his favorite player had developed circulation problems that required amputation. After hours of these types of "testing" Milt was satisfied I was not acquiring thoughts from his mind but that spirit indeed was supplying me with accurate information.

As validating as this process was it still didn't satisfy my desire to understand how this gift would serve God. This experience was exciting but it still left an uneasiness in my being. I still needed to know how and if this ability was of God and would serve God. Again, I went directly to the Source asking, "OK God. If all this activity is of Your making, prove it to me so there is not a shred of doubt in my mind that it's OK to pursue.

His answer came the following week in the

form of a newly developed business associate and eventual dear friend, Dr. Colene Allen. It was a miraculous happening, and I'll now let Colene share her story as outlined in her book, Welcome Back Little Child.

Chapter Seven

Welcome Back Little Child
Colene Allen's Story

My life was about to be turned upside down, yet I was totally unaware of the forces already in motion. Forces that required the courage and caring of two strangers, my open heart and mind, all brought together by the exquisite timing only God can produce.

It was not the kind of business meeting you'd expect. Susan and Milt Sanderford and I met in May of 1995 to arrange a trade-out promotion between their newspaper, The Mirror, and radio station WOKB where I was general manager. WOKB was introducing new programming of the Personal Achievement Network, featuring motivational giants like Dennis Waitley, Zig Ziglar, and Anthony Robbins, and also to introduce our radio audience to the positive good-news newspaper of Central Florida—The Mirror. Susan was the Mirror's owner and publisher, and Milt the managing editor.

Instantly I realized Susan and Milt had special qualities. After exchanging pleasantries, it was also clear they were Christians. "What exceptional people," I thought. Unexplainably, I felt particularly bonded to Susan.

Early in the meeting I was uncharacteristically moved to mention my involvement in massage therapy and non-traditional healing through the power of the Holy Spirit. Definitely not your run of the mill business talk.

As I shared with Milt and Susan how God had been working in my life, Susan began to cry. Instinctively feeling God must have done something special in her life, I said, "You must have had a real awakening?" "You've got that right!" Milt responded with a broad smile. A business associate then joined us and our talk quickly moved to the business at hand.

As the brief meeting came to an end, feeling that something of great importance was being set in motion, I told Susan it would be nice to get together on a personal basis. She agreed and we went our separate ways without special plans being made.

As they drove home, Susan was so filled with unexplained emotion she was left speechless for a long period. Telling Milt she didn't understand why, but she felt something special was about to happen, and there was a special reason for me being in their life. Little did any of us know how accurate she was, and how dramatically the revelation would come.

Several weeks later while sorting through neglected mail on my desk, I picked up a letter Susan had written on May 12, 1995. She closed by saying, "On a personal note, thank you for your openness in sharing yourself. God answered a prayer in our meeting. I sensed that you were yet another validation to the truths that God has been revealing to me over the past several weeks. As you suggested, I would enjoy meeting with you on a personal basis."

As I laid the letter on my desk the phone rang. It was Susan with an invitation to meet her and Milt for dinner. I felt comfortable in accepting. We agreed on Tuesday, July 11.

Susan called on July 10 to confirm our date. With so many things occurring in my life since we last talked, I had almost forgotten the engagement. As though in a fog, and not knowing why, I had scrawled her name on my notepad three times earlier that very day. We chatted a few minutes and confirmed the appointment for the next evening.

Unfortunately, the next day, realizing

time was running out and needing to face up to a difficult task, I felt unable to keep the appointment. In twelve days, my husband and I would be leaving Orlando as Dan had recently accepted a dream-come-true position in Pueblo, Colorado. Painful as it would be preparing for the move, I could no longer postpone sorting through my daughter's personal items.

Almost five agonizing years ago, my beautiful and precious seventeen-year-old, Donna Lynda Lynn, took her life — leaving a vast void in mine. My pain and confusion continued over the years, causing many tears and unbearable heartache.

Questions continually haunted my mind: Why? Why did she do it? Why did it happen?

Didn't she realize the finality of such an action? Didn't she realize the pain it would cause? What might I have done to prevent such a drastic solution to her pain?

On the 11th, I called Milt to explain my need to cancel our engagement and reschedule for Thursday, July 13. His acceptance was gracious. For some reason, I assumed the get together was for business purposes, a follow-up to our first brief meeting. After all, we didn't know each other personally. Milt explained to me the meeting was personal, not of a business nature—not connected with the radio station. That interested me all the more. It was a warm invitation, and even though immersed in the painful sorting and packing process, I was becoming excited about what might be going on.

Chapter Eight

Believe or not to believe
Was that the question?

Thursday my husband's car wound up in the shop. When Milt called to confirm our dinner, I told him I wouldn't be able to attend due to a lack of transportation. With urgency in his voice, he wouldn't hear of another postponement, offering to pick me up after work. It was obvious he felt we needed to meet this very night.

Greeting as though old friends, I was happy to see them again. With a sense of pleasant anticipation, we drove to a nearby restaurant, chatting about my husband's and my recent decision to move to Colorado, my excitement about the move and the hard work involved in uprooting after living in Orlando my entire life.

During dinner Milt asked questions about my healing interest and about my faith in general. They were personal questions asked in such a way as to please, most certainly not to frighten or cause defensiveness. Once Milt sensed we were both comfortable with the conversational direction, he asked my views on "channeling", and communication with the spirit world.

As a little girl, I was taught by church, and family members, that things of that sort were evil, therefore I had a bit of built-in bias against it. However, I was never certain those negative messages were well founded, being well aware that many people have unexplained special gifts. Since I had not yet experienced the phenomenon, and hesitating to get involved because of the way I was conditioned, I remained closed and a bit fearful.

Upon reflection, I realized a number of unexplained phenomena had already occurred in my life, a part of which was the fact that I had healing ability and an awareness of things before they happen. My intuition tells me about different things. Whether in their presence or not, at times I have the ability to know either about a person's past, present or sometimes their future.

As God points out in 1 Corinthians, Chapter 12, "He has given us all different abilities," and this particular day God was about to show me a new one. The neat thing about this, and all I've been learning since I opened my heart to Christ and dedicated my life to Him 100 percent, is that God is sending people to instruct me in different areas, one at a time, in His own time, showing me the spiritual aspects that go with it, and it has been so comfortable, enlightening, fantastic and right!

Milt went on to explain about channeling, giving me clear insight, which let me know that God was indeed talking through him, letting me know that this was an OK thing. Raised from infancy in the church, he told me how direct communication with the Holy Spirit and spirit world in general was a foreign concept to him, neither hearing pro nor con from the pulpit.

Exposed to the world of psychic phenomena in his late forties, Milt described himself as a strong skeptic—until a dramatic experience changed his thinking. At the age of thirty-two, his wife Mary Jane died after a two-year struggle with leukemia.

A chance comment to the owner of a multi-million dollar national sales organization initiated a chain of events that lead to undeniable contact with his wife 30-days after her death. The story was beautiful and fascinating.

As he shared these things with me I could feel that Milt was a very loving person, a very humble person, and being around him and listening to him talk — I could feel the Spirit of Christ around him, and I could feel the Holy

Spirit. It was a great and sensational feeling. I knew intuitively that Milt was in a very close walk with God.

While Milt was talking I noticed Susan appeared anxious about something, while at the same time positive and excited. I could also feel the love of God she has—a very special warmth. It's unspoken but very beautiful warmth that she projects, and I noticed it the very first time I met her.

I could sense her mixture of frustration and excitement, as though she was involved in a tug-of-war with... How am I going to do this? Will she accept it? I want to do this, I have to do this, I'm going to do this, and I know that God is with me!

She showed me in her actions, even without speaking, that she is very close to God. I know with all my heart that God is going to use her mightily, and I feel that fact with strength and certainty. I can also tell that Susan is very cautious of what she says and what she does, thinking before she speaks.

At this point I was a bit confused because I wasn't sure what my role was in this particular situation, and why they were talking to me about these things. All I knew was it seemed comfortable and right! I knew that God had a message for me here and now, and as His child, I had to patiently and intently listen for it.

Chapter Nine

To Make a Point

With sincerity and conviction, Susan explained that within the past several weeks God had chosen her to act as His channel to assist in spiritual healing for those believers in need. Although just beginning to receive "how-to" instruction from spirit, she was already able to channel needed information from spirit to believers.

Like most of us brought up in the Christian church, these things were never accepted as being from God, indeed, many times our "teachers" led us to believe they were a product of evil. Because of this, Susan was understandably apprehensive about what this assignment from God would require of her—facing judgment by many, the possible loss of friends and family, indeed the likelihood of an extremely lonely walk.

Susan felt God's voice and plans for her life were unmistakable and undeniable. There was no way she was about to turn her back on

Him, just to fit into the limiting regulations and thought process of those not totally surrendered to God.

What an amazing coincidence that this woman who sat before me, had surrendered her entire being to God's will and direction just as I had done, in the exact month, October of 1993, crying out in frustration, "God, if you are out there, take me and mold me after your will— for this life I am leading is empty and lonely without You!" From that time on, miracle upon miracle had come Susan's way, being freed from an unhappy marriage, learning of God's true plan for love, and now this special gift to develop and use to help others, in His name, and to His glory.

As the evening progressed it became obvious to me Susan had truly been touched and chosen by God, and that He will lead those people to her who can benefit from this exceptional and miraculous talent.

Susan went on to tell me that a few weeks prior she was given a clear image of me while praying. She saw me dance across the floor as a graceful ballerina wearing a black dress. I had long blond hair and was very beautiful and graceful. For someone who had only met me once it seemed to me odd she would be praying for me, or even thinking about me.

I was shocked at the information. When I

was six years old I wanted to be a ballerina. My cousin, Carla was taking lessons and my mother agreed to let Jan, my adopted sister, attend a tryout practice.

I had gone several times but was rather clumsy. As they chose a line of girls to be in a play, we were to audition for a spot. Jan's mom Voncille, the lady who adopted me when my mother died when I was seven, made me a black tutu outfit. I had long curly blond hair — and although so very ungainly, in my heart I was that beautiful ballerina flying through the air.

It startled me that Susan saw this because there are only two people alive that would know anything about this part of my life. This to me was just a phenomenal validation that, whoever was passing on these details to Susan, knew my life very well. As this story unfolds, I can now fully understand and accept that God put His hand on her, to get a much-needed message to me!

Susan revealed she had spent time praying for me that afternoon, making notes on a number of things that appeared during her meditation. She had no idea what they meant or how they related to me, but felt she had been asked to share them. Keep in mind, Susan didn't know me, nor did she know anyone related to me. As she spoke each item, I immediately knew the exact meaning of each. There were several items that I knew absolutely no one could have told her about, since I had never shared these things with anyone.

Referring to her pre-typed list, Susan began to share what had been given her by someone in spirit. She first saw a young woman as a ballerina, feeling this was a validation that the information she was about to receive was "addressed" to me. (As she had seen me a few weeks earlier as a ballerina.)

Susan was then given the name Joann. "Who is Joann?" Milt asked. I was so surprised they would know my adopted sister's name. Joann is actually my first cousin, the "Jan" with whom I grew up. She was my mom's best friend, staying with us quite a bit while I was growing up.

Susan saw a left hand with a ring on it, and a female hand with dark fingernail polish. She described in detail the type of ring I was wearing on my left hand and the nail polish I was wearing that evening—very strange since I constantly change my nail polish.

She then saw a big bell ringing. She felt that meant to focus on the ring. She was then shown what the ring looked like. The ring is unusual, with a great deal of personal meaning to me. An emerald in an oblong star shape, with tiny diamonds around it having three bands of gold that come off of it, a point on one end and it dips to a point on the other end. The ring was a gift from my husband when we married, but it's also meaningful because emeralds are very important to me. It was a ring that originally contained my birthstone, an amethyst, but the stone kept falling out. When he took it back to the jewelers, he replaced the stone. The amazing part is Susan had so accurately ascribed this ornate ring—all written down before she ever saw it.

Next she saw two hands lifting up what looked like a ball of energy. We both instinctively knew this represented the healing energies I have been given. As the healing ball was lifted up, it grew larger and larger, apparently indicating expansion in this area.

She then saw two hands pushing away from the hands of a nun. Susan, felt this was me pushing away from the nun. I then shared with Milt and Susan that when I was young I attended Catholic Church and school. They were very strict and when I became a young mother I left the Catholic Church, not comfortable with the degree of strictness.

Milt then asked if the name Mary Beth meant anything to me. Susan had been given this name. Mary Beth was Marilyn Beth, my mother-in-law. Susan mentioned a wedding dress and wedding bells in connection with her. My mother-in-law and I had been discussing the fact that she could be married in my wedding dress if a current relationship developed to that point.

Susan then mentioned seeing an old woman dragging her foot, saying "come-to-me." I did not connect with this on right away, but later it proved to very interesting when I understood who she was. I began to understand that this wealth of personal information passed on through Susan was to establish the validity of both the sender and the message that was about to follow. Obviously, it was from one who was extremely close to me—knowing me very well.

The name Mark was given and I was astonished. Mark was my deceased husband. Susan then saw three lit candles sitting on a table, feeling this symbolized three people that were connected with me. I knew immediately, it represented three people very close to me who had all passed away. The lit candles seemed to say they were still alive, "Their light was still burning!"

Susan then saw a diamond ring. As she watched, the diamond grew larger. The engagement ring my husband Dan gave me had a small diamond. He recently had this diamond replaced with a larger diamond. It did indeed "grow" from small to large. In connection with this she also saw wedding bells and someone in a wedding dress.

The last thing she saw was the ballerina again, and I felt this was telling her that all these images were validations for me that someone in spirit was trying to reach me through Susan.

Then the bombshell exploded! With sensitive smiling eyes, Milt asked how many children did I have, and if one was in spirit. It was then that I told them, for the first time, of my daughter Donna Lynda Lynn, who had committed suicide five years ago and whose passing I was still mourning. His words struck a chord of truth when he said "Colene, we believe all this information was passed on to Susan from Donna Lynda Lynn. We feel she wants — needs to talk with you directly!"

Chapter Ten

The Reunion

Milt went on to say that during Susan's meditation, he asked Lynda for some additional validation so I would more readily accept that it was she who was making this contact. That's when Lynda said Mark was with her (remember, this was passed on to Susan and Milt from Lynda, and written down some five hours before I ever told them my husband Mark was deceased, and so also was my beloved Lynda), and she also shared her awareness that I was moving to Colorado—but she knew I was having difficulty with the move because I had to sort through her belongings, and because I would be leaving that place where I last spoke and held my Lynda.

When Milt asked Lynda if she wanted to pursue direct contact with me through Susan, she said she would. I could not eat another bite. Although in a state of shock, it felt so loving, so right, and so very much needed. My daughter had been directed to seek out this clear channel, to address both our needs. My heart filled with positive anticipation. I asked Susan and Milt if they would be willing to come to my house at this time, to which they both agreed. We left immediately for the house.

When we reached my home, I first took them into the garage, which had been converted, to a family room, showing Susan a collage of pictures of Lynda. Susan emitted an immediate gasp of recognition saying, "That's the beautiful girl I saw, except her hair was longer, curly and pulled back like this!", taking her hands and fixing her hair in the exact style as was Lynda's hair the day of her death. Lynda had just had her hair permed the week before. Susan had not remembered this information she had seen when she was meditating earlier, but as soon as she saw Lynda's picture the description of her came pouring out.

Susan went on to describe the position of the body when found. It was exactly as she envisioned, as was Susan's description of Lynda's clothing and makeup on the day she died. Yet another validation as to how clear and pure were Susan's channeling abilities.

With deliberate anticipatory strides,

the three of us walked down the hall and into Lynda's room, the room in which she committed suicide. As the door was opened, we entered, each of us sensing a presence in the room beyond the obvious three.

After a few seconds of observation, we joined hands as Susan began by saying a prayer of guidance and protection for her, Milt, and myself. "Father, we ask for your direction and guidance. As we open up to spirit, we ask that only good will be allowed in this room. We ask for your protection and that you surround us with your perfect love and light. We pray this in Jesus' name. Amen."

No sooner had the prayer ended and our hands released their hold on each other, Susan took on an entirely different personality. With forceful gestures and a highly emotional voice, Susan began to channel. I could see the pain in her face, the same pain in Lynda. It cannot be more accurately described in words—but the look on her face was the identical look my daughter would get when she was in such excruciating pain.

One of the things Lynda said in her final letter to me was she just could not stand the pain anymore. The poor child experienced so much pain when she had these headaches and traumas. Medication seemed never able to help. (Lithium and Thorazine were two of the medications.) As Susan began to talk, there were things that were said that left not a shred of doubt it was my daughter talking to me. I had no doubt it was my daughter speaking through Susan.

"Mommy, I am so sorry!", were the first words from Susan's mouth, as she held out her arms to me in emotional gesturing. My daughter always said "Mommy" to me when she was in a great deal of pain or really hurting and wanting my special attention. At other times, she always called me "Mom" or "Mother" after becoming a teenager. But when hurt or suffering, she always reverted to "Mommy"! The expression on Susan's face, the tone of voice, and the way she pronounced the words—these were all identical to my daughter, it left me speechless, knowing it was my daughter coming through this beautiful God-filled woman. You mothers know what I mean when you know how your child sounds, and then is taken away from you, and you hear that same sound again— it immediately grabs your senses. You would never forget it not even a little bit.

The next thing she said was "Mommy, I didn't

mean to hurt you so bad! I'm so sorry. I'm so, so sorry. I didn't realize Mommy. I didn't mean to hurt you like that!" When my daughter was very ill, when she would go through difficult stages requiring hospitalization, she would experience blackouts, becoming very violent. After the incidents, she would coil into a tight fetal position, rocking back and forth crying "Mommy, I'm so, so sorry, I'm so, so sorry. I didn't mean it, I didn't mean to hurt you, I'm so, so sorry!"

The way Susan was talking was exactly the same pattern Lynda used. There was no doubt this was Lynda. Susan (Lynda) then kept repeating, "The pain was so bad, the pain was so bad, I couldn't take the pain." My daughter used to say that to me so often. And understand this, Susan had never met my daughter and did not know me, or anyone who knew my daughter or me.

To me this is important to understand because it was all so clear to me that my daughter was actually communicating to me through one of God's servants, Susan Sanderford, a pure and beautiful person who offered herself to God and to His work. Never asking — only giving, giving one of the most precious gifts I could never imagine to ask for.

Lynda continued in her distressful voice, "The pain, it hurt so bad, the pain it hurt so bad!" I could actually SEE my daughter—as she used to look. Her hair was a little longer, her makeup was just perfect, and she was just beautiful. She had on her red and white dress, absolutely gorgeous.

I could see through her. It was as if she was standing in front of Susan, not to her side. I could see Susan, but I could also see Lynda right in front of her, exactly the way she was dressed the day she killed herself.

It was then that I finally spoke to her, "Did you realize when you did this, the pain you were going to cause—that you would no longer be here with me? Did you know what was going to happen to you?" She said, "No Mommy, I didn't realize... the pain was just so bad. I just wanted to stop the hurt Mommy. I just wanted to stop the hurt. I feel so bad Mommy. I can't go mommy, I can't move on, because I need you to forgive me." "God has forgiven me and mommy, I want you to forgive me." I told her that I loved her very much, she was my daughter and she would always be a part of me no matter what—and I would never ever NOT forgive her because I loved her so much." She responded, "Mommy, I'm happy here. I'm here with daddy Mark and daddy Steve, and I'm happy here Mommy. I just need you to forgive me. I just need your forgiveness."

I said, "Yes Lynda, I forgive you. I forgive you with all my heart." The next thing that came out was "Mommy, please don't forget me, please don't forget me. I'm so afraid you'll forget me." This really struck me hard because on Sunday night before she passed away, Lynda had questioned me so much on this one subject.

"Mommy, when people die, do you forget them? Do you ever forget them? Do they stay with you or do they leave you, or what happens to them? Talk to me about it!" I explained to her that no, you don't forget people when they die. You continue to love them, it's just that they are not there every day, and you might not think about them every day, but you don't always think about loved ones every day when they're here either.

You just don't forget people that you love. So, this statement coming out of Susan's mouth was so identical to what Lynda had asked me the night before her death. I can't explain the chills that overtook me.

I told my daughter that I would always love

her and that she would always be a part of me. There was no way I could ever forget her, but that she had to move on, she had to go into the light, and as I spoke those words, she turned to walk into the light and held out her hand. Susan saw something that looked like a heart in Lynda's hand and she said, "I will go into the light, but I will always be with you!"

My beautiful child peacefully turned and walked slowly into the light, both Susan and I seeing her walking away.

Chapter Eleven

The Release

Suddenly everything came into focus. Several nights before, Dan told me a light coming from Lynda's bedroom had awakened him. Two nights later, we both were awakened by an extremely, bright light emanating from that same room. No streetlight could be that bright. It scared him. He also shared the fact that when we would have a minor argument from time to time, he received the distinct feeling someone else was in the room looking at him. This sensation made him feel very uncomfortable.

Our house had been up for sale since January without a single inquiry being received. No one looked at it, no one showed interest in it. I honestly feel Lynda somehow had a hold on the house, was bound to the house, needing to experience closure with me.

The morning she died I walked past her

room and saw Lynda cuddled up in a white blanket, her beautiful blond hair falling across her face, her arm dangling on the ground. She looked so beautiful and peaceful, I thought—like an angel.

When I returned to the house after her death, I could see a beautiful golden light stretching down from above—and I sensed she had probably died before the bullet even struck her. I felt her spirit likely left the physical body before it could feel the pain.

I also felt the presence of another entity in the room. It was a dark entity, and I felt that God had taken her spirit before this darker entity could have gotten to her. I've often wondered if that entity was a friend of Lynda's who had died several months before her death. He had tried several times to talk her into committing suicide with him. This was not her first attempt.

Sadly, she could never explain where her pain came from, nor could the doctors ever learn its origin. Lynda left a beautiful note to me and underlined several times, "This is not your fault, and I love you very, very, very much."

One of the things my daughter said as she turned to walk into the light is, "Mommy, you'll be OK—Go with Dan!" Since Susan had not been told my husband's name, this gave even stronger evidence that Lynda actually knew that I was leaving, and she needed to come to me before I could leave. She also knew, if I left before we had the opportunity to settle things between us, she would have been "stuck" here.

I don't remember the exact words, but with the wedding dress and ring, she was showing to Susan during the initial contact—I feel she was telling me she attended our wedding and was pleased. She even said, "You need to go with Dan, everything is going to be all right now. Wherever you go, my heart will always be with you!"

Instantaneously it was like the weight of the world had been lifted off of the house, and my shoulders. Miraculously, the very next day we had five calls for appointments to show the house, resulting in one possible sale. It was incredible—just incredible!

When the channeling of Lynda ended, Susan seemed about to cry, and I know she had literally experienced the heaviness and sadness Lynda had felt. Interestingly, I could hear my daughter speak a second or two before Susan uttered her words. During that time, I could so strongly feel her presence—I could even smell her!

I cannot explain to you how to smell a person, but when you are with someone continuously, you may not realize they have their unique smell, and when gone, you can pick up a piece of their clothing or a pillow, and you smell their presence. I knew it was Lynda—I could hear her, I could see her and I could smell her. It was an amazing process. And it took this reunion to free her to progress to where she needed to go, while also freeing me to move forward, free of pain, it released a number of things and helped heal a lot of things.

Likely it doesn't always happen to everyone who dies, but especially in suicides, where their spirit is kind of lost and needs to do, or say, something final because they did not realize the consequences of what they were doing and did not have the opportunity to say what they needed to say—yet they now need to move on for further healing and spiritual growth.

Once all this was accomplished through Susan, it set the house free, it set Lynda free, and it most certainly set me free! Today is a brighter day for me. It has helped me a great deal and I feel like it was a perfect ending to a bad story—a story that became a beautiful flower.

No sooner than Lynda moved on and Susan, Milt and I embraced, basking in the love and warmth of the poignant farewell, I became overpowered and speechless, sensing the presence of someone else in the room. I tried to speak but my voice was choking on the attempted words. I wanted to tell Susan someone else was here with something to say, but the words wouldn't come.

Chapter Twelve

Farewell but not goodbye

As a young girl of five, I had an imaginary Indian friend. We did a number of fun things together. It was then I developed a passion for birds—especially the eagle, along with the ability to pick up injured birds, touch them in love and they would be healed. I also touched other wounded animals and they were healed.

To satisfy my love for birds, my dad bought a number of chickens for me to care for. Sharing this interest with my Indian friend, he, in turn, shared his eagle with me. I used to feel it was a part of me.

I felt I could actually fly when I jumped off of things, the strangest of realistic sensations. That was a sweet and simple time of life, a time of accepting, not questioning. The amazing part is I could literally sit for hours and talk with this imaginary friend.

My mother died when I was seven, so I

went to live with my grandparents, aunts and uncles. What a difficult time in my life, struggling with mother's death, my passage into womanhood, dealing with being so much taller than the other girls. To complicate matters, I had a great deal more responsibility than other children my age. With all the stress and negativity, I still only missed three days of school. It was then that I felt my Indian friend was sent to watch over me, to keep me in good health. Naively, I told my family and friends I could see my Indian friend thus I was teased continually—then "warned" about him. We went to a Baptist church and a Church of God, and they both made me feel very scared of God. Unfortunately. they taught me to fear God. I feel that's why so many people are afraid to be Christians, and why some people do cruel dumb things, all in the name of Christianity. (Note: when my parents were living, we were Catholic.)

Thankfully, I now understand that "God is Love." But as a child, these "Christian" people caused me to be so frightened of God, I would do whatever they asked because I feared God's punishment and being sent to hell if I didn't follow their instructions. When I became a teenager, the pressure mounted. I was ridiculed, made to be frightened about my Indian friend, being told he was not of God.

Sadly, I decided to just let go of my Indian friend, although I had a strong sense he tried to hold onto me. In retrospect, he must have continued to watch over me because I so rarely had an illness. I had a continual sense someone was indeed watching over me.

Now my eight-year-old grandson has an imaginary friend and I know exactly why he has it. It's such a shame we teach children fear, causing them to lose that childlike belief and faith. When children are children, they are open and honest, not afraid of anything, and moving forward with enthusiasm. I have come to understand that so much was lost in my life because I was taught fear, instead of God's love.

Now I understand why my Indian friend returned this past year, and I know where he's coming from. I always thought he was perhaps a part of my higher self since I was taught not to believe in spirits. Then Susan and Milt unveiled yet another beautiful experience to me, helping me to realize my "imaginary" friend was not imaginary after all. Nor was he a part of my subconscious, acting as my higher self. He is my spirit guide. This is all a major part of understanding—a new beginning that started with his return in 1994.

Chapter Thirteen

Face to face with an old friend

"There is someone here wishing to make contact. A spirit of tremendous power!" Susan proclaimed, as she reverted to her channeling mode. Almost simultaneously I was aware of his presence.

Then, I saw my spirit guide come to me. He is a very old, old man dressed in pelts of animal skins sewn together in a floor-length cloak. A band of eagle feathers dangles behind his left shoulder. His long course gray hair hangs below his shoulders, and his gentle eyes are gray in color. His complexion is a dark Indian-olive color, with beautifully weathered skin. He wears turquoise bracelets on both arms with what appear to be pearl and garnet stones. Standing about six feet tall, with a thin body, he also carries a long spear with many feathers and an animal pelt on it.

The first time I remember seeing him since

bidding farewell as a child, was in 1994. It was then I began to redevelop the gift of healing.

A gentleman I worked with had lung cancer at 35 years of age, having been given six-months to live. Using the Holy Spirit healing energy, my Indian friend was right there showing me what to do and telling me what to say. Although I had a bit of a problem accepting it at the time, this is when my Indian friend reappeared to me and told me how to handle the situation.

I made a cassette tape instructing the types of foods to eat, prayers to pray and positive affirmations to use. I also told him he needed to rid himself of resentment and anger toward his biological father. That man was totally healed and has remained so for a year. This was my first healing experience since I was a young girl healing the animals.

After this wondrous experience, I began calling my Indian friend my "shaman" (medicine man). I have seen my shaman several times after this and he enters through a very purple haze encircled by the most beautiful light of gold, best described as gold on red. He comes closer and closer until I feel his touch as he stands by my side.

My shaman appeared as Susan began to speak, bringing with him my beautiful golden eagle. As he approached, the eagle was on his right shoulder. He extended his right arm and the eagle walked down his arm, spreading its wings and flew to me. I mentally reached my arm out and the eagle landed and walked up to my shoulder.

The feeling that came over me at that moment was of great power. As Susan reached over to hold my hand to steady me, she said she felt intense power course through her own body. Power to a degree she had never before experienced.

As Susan began channeling the message my Shaman had for me, I could see the eagle leave me and fly to her. "Your eagle is now coming to me" Susan shared. She could actually see the eagle as this was happening, then it left her to fly back to me. I instantly knew that this was my shaman's way of showing me that Susan and I were connected — that she was the accepted channel for him, letting me know that I should listen and verbally hear what he was going to say through her.

Susan began to speak, "They are here to tell you that you have been given great healing powers. Your healing powers are about to expand even further and your mind must be more open to new abilities of healing. We will be helping you develop your healing abilities. Do not discard what you have learned already, but open yourself to other thoughts and forms of healing!" Then he was gone.

As she began to say these things I realized I had heard these messages before, not from other people, but through my inner voice. I knew exactly what was meant. The power in that room was overwhelming—almost overpowering. Their message came through loud and clear, and I was receiving and accepting.

Finally, I now knew he was not an imaginary friend, but a true spirit guide, helping to teach what God is wanting to do with me, and for me. He was guiding me. Whatever one calls him, a soldier of God or a servant of God, I see God in my shaman. A spirit sent by God to aid in spiritual growth, development and service to others.

Chapter Fourteen

Welcome back little child

As soon as my shaman left, the room felt quiet and peaceful. Milt, Susan and I were totally amazed at what had just happened. Not only had I been reunited with Lynda, I also was given a powerful nod of approval to continue on the path of healing. I could now leave Orlando knowing that Lynda was at peace, I was at peace, and would be using my healing gift with the assistance of my "Indian friend" to help others on their spiritual journey.

What a great sense of relaxation we all felt—a job well done. An important mission completed. For the first time since Lynda's death the house was so open and fresh.

Susan, Milt and I spent the next half hour basking in the glow of that which had just taken place. I could not thank them enough for their love, concern and gift so freely given. I could not thank God enough for bringing it all about in His perfect timing.

I felt completely at ease in letting go of such a negative burden, and gaining so much peace and joy in return, experiencing the release and closure so often spoken of and written about. It was accomplished, allowing Lynda to move forward on her spiritual journey, and me to progress with mine free of the sorrowful weight that held us both back.

There is not a doubt in my mind this is how God blesses those of His children who surrender themselves to Him, bringing peace that passes all understanding into their lives. For those of you who feel God's miracles are connected to ancient times, or more "traditional" ways, I can tell you His miracles continue to abound daily—my miracle being a witness to that truth.

It was like I was back as that little child again, my child — ME. The little person that I used to be, filled with faith and wonder, I was back totally and fully. For through these contacts with those in spirit, a monumental healing had taken place.

I listen to my intuition so much, and I know if I follow it I will do the right thing because it is God's voice through spirit. If I hear it and go against it, things will not flow in a positive or orderly fashion. Wisely, I chose to go with it!

What a wonderful gift from God, it was clear

explanation and validation, an undeniable answer that channeling was indeed a tool for good, for healing, from God. However, I continue to strongly feel you need to constantly be on guard when dealing with spirit contact, that there are channels and spirits you don't want to become involved with.

If God is bringing it to you in this manner, through people like Susan and Milt, it is safe, meaningful, healing and reliable. By their fruits ye shall know them!

Chapter Fifteen

The Ripple Effect

I met with Susan and Milt for a farewell lunch on the following Thursday, confirming with them some additional miraculous happenings resulting from their approaching me with God's healing touch. They'll never know how much this meant to me, for words are inadequate to describe.

Susan shared that my shaman had come, again, to her at 3:00 a.m. the morning after our experience. She saw a lone wolf howling and was told my Indian guide's name was "Lone Wolf". The message he passed on to Susan at that time was for me to be, "open to study Indian forms of healing". I was excited to hear this, since the area to which we were moving was rich in Native-American History.

As confirmation of his name, I had also received an impression that same day that "Lone Wolf" was indeed his name. What fun when Susan called to give me his name, and

I was able to say, "I know, I know, it is Lone Wolf!"

I now also understand who the old woman dragging her foot was. She is my great grandmother who is also in spirit. I was told, "she will lead me where I need to go, she will guide." She does not speak to me, but is there to show me the way.

The blessings received from Susan's channeling of Lynda, Lone Wolf and other spirit guides were more than I could ask for— yet within days, the healing process continued to ripple outward through my family.

I was able to speak with my daughter Michelle, my sister Eva, and my adopted sister JoAnn (Jan). We sat at Eva's home, in the living room, as Eva and Jan shared experiences with me they had never told me because they saw how I had been treated by the family. They were such wonderful things to talk about.

Eva told how she had asked God if she could see our Mother. She was two years old when our Mother committed suicide. Her biological father was my stepfather, who adopted me at 18 months old. Mom died in April, he died in November the same year, so she did not know either of them.

Eva said mom appeared at the foot of our

bed, she described in detail her dress and how she looked. I remembered that dress. She said, "Mom appeared to be in a light, standing on a stage, illuminating the room." And she told Eva to ask all the questions she wanted and she would answer them. Since this is Eva's story, I will only say I could identify with the story as being a true account.

Jan then told about her father, (my Uncle, and also the Uncle that adopted Eva and me after the death of our parents), who had passed away in January — this is now July. She told how he came to her in human form, kissed her, talked with her and gave her information. When the conversation ended he was gone.

I had already shared my story earlier.

My daughter Michelle was startled by all this, having never experienced it. Yet, she listened intently and made the comment, "So Aunt Eva and Aunt Jan you both have had these experiences; and you knew my mom had had experiences many times; and you never told these stories, because mom had been mistreated and called names and even punished for this?" The answer from both of them at the same time was, "yes".

Having them confirm to me that they too had gifts really inspired my heart's desire to never lose this ability again.

I had a friend who worked with me at the Radio Station, WOKB; he was a minister, a healer, a psychic-medium, he was well known and worked with people like John Edward, Tony Robbins and others. His name is Jason L. Oliver. He had been working with me in my psychic abilities and allowing myself to see these abilities in the form of a gift from God. He had been encouraging me for several months, and working with me to overcome other things in life. I had not been ready or willing to go to the level of working on family stuff, or my daughter's death. He just kept saying the time would come. He had developed "Whole Life Integration" and had it patented in 1989. It is a wonderful form of healing for both sides. He and I were very close friends.

My husband Dan was not fond of hearing about any of this. He was excited we were leaving Florida in hopes of getting me away from such things. Little did either of us realize, this was just the beginning.

On the way to Colorado, as I drove with my dog Soupy, in one vehicle, my husband Dan was in the truck pulling the UHAUL. I taped this story, sent it to Milt to review and compare to his recollection. After being put in typed format, it has been given to many people to help overcome their fears from loss of loved ones.

I tried to accommodate my husband by being very quiet about my gifts, but they kept growing. It became an impossibility to keep quiet. Clients came from all over, I did very little advertising and people received the healing they needed.

It is such a wonderful thing to be a part of someone's healing experience. And when you help another heal, you too have healing given back.

Eva has a thriving flower shop business in a very small town, mainly dealing in funeral displays. She uses her gift in a different way through her personal expressions in her work, guided by those passed on. She is able to say things, make special arrangements to their loved ones and answers questions that only the one passed could convey. It has helped her become successful, not just in our hometown, but all over the southern states, to help those who call for some of her exquisite special orders for funerals, for people and animals alike.

Jan received the answers she needed to fulfill completion of schooling as an audiologist just after turning 62 years old. Helping people communicate, not only in hearing, but being around elders who she could console about the losses of family and friends in her own way as well. But without the help of the spirit of the deceased she would not have had any way to truly help these people.

My daughter began to understand that her son had a gift and did not ridicule him, but allowed him to develop his gifts. As well, she now understands me better, and her Aunts. She began to see a world much greater than the one she saw before. Her faith became stronger and she has grown in so many ways.

My grandson is no longer afraid to be himself and searches out how, and when, to use his gifts of the spirit. He too will continue to grow.

I know there is to be a special closeness between Susan and me. Even though we will be miles apart, I sense a beautiful and unbreakable bond has developed between us, and interesting and beneficial things will result. God does indeed work in mysterious ways, and he certainly had a meaningful and beautiful purpose in bringing us together.

God has given Susan such a beautiful gift all because she is a special person in His sight, a surrendered and pure channel, willing to work for Him. I know He will bring many to her. Her gift will help these people face and overcome difficult spiritual and earthly problems connected to spirit. As she has done in mine, as an agent of God, she will bring true healing into their lives.

Many will judge this gift not to be of God, and that's OK. It is not for all to understand and accept. Many believers have a great deal of maturing to accomplish before they reach this level of God's outpouring of abundance. It is certainly not for those who made gods of their church buildings, rules and regulations and look-down-the-nose attitude toward anyone who has a different concept of God's truth and love.

As in my life, Susan's and Milt's life, we all doubted and had negative feelings toward this kind of activity early on. We were conditioned to believe that way. We continually thank God for the strength to have persevered, to move beyond the small minds who put God in a convenient pigeonhole, to use Him as it serves what they wish to expose.

Isn't it interesting how each of us had similar experiences in the church, and beyond. We took our love of God, appreciation for Christ Jesus' life, death and resurrection, the knowledge gained from the Holy Spirit, and went a step beyond the average Christian's willingness—surrendering all to God, asking Him to mold us and make us after His own will. That's when the blessings began to flow in each of our lives. That's when He took us to a higher level of understanding. That, my friends, is not a coincidence. It is a fulfilment of God's promise.

As their relationship deepens and blossoms, and as they continue to seek and serve the Lord, I know Susan and Milt will be used mightily for God. Each of them has already been directed by the Holy Spirit to begin writing their experiences targeted toward searching believers. I continually pray for them both.

Colene Allen

Chapter Sixteen

Proof received and acknowledged

A powerful retelling Colene. Thank you for being the agent of God's response to my asking Him to prove this gift would be used only to His honor and to benefit those who were in pain or in a search for HIM.

Well, that powerful healing experience took place well over twenty years ago and since then husband Milt and I have traveled far and wide throughout the world, facilitated many spiritual growth workshops and retreats, conducted thousands of spirit communication and spiritual growth healing phone consultations, presented numerous Tele-Seminars, along with writing a book or two along the way.

Milt and I live a modest and satisfying life, still following spirit's leading. At this very moment in December of 2017 we are here in Colorado having long ago accepted Jesus' request to create a place of healing and spiritual growth in San Luis, Colorado, Jesus named it Casa de Santa Maria—explaining "It's where my Mother's healing presence will reside along with her holy helpers."

I'll guarantee you one thing, if you decide to surrender your life to God, prepare for an interesting, sometimes tumultuous yet fulfilling experience.

To my wonderful partner in this adventure, thanks for your unconditional love, ancient yet relevant wisdom, unending support, amazing sense of humor and beautiful sense of life! It wouldn't have been the same without you dear Milt Sanderford—in fact, it couldn't have happened without you.

The Beginning
Susan Sanderford

Epilogue

Since this documented healing through spirit communication experience with Colene Allen, following spirit's request Susan and Milt Sanderford have traveled to sacred sites throughout the world including;

- Eight roundtrips to Australia that involved;

- A pilgrimage to Uluru deep within the Australian outback.

- Living two years in Byron Bay, Australia.

- Three pilgrimages to Medjugorje, Bosnia.

- A pilgrimage to Abadiania, Brazil..

- A pilgrimage to Ground Zero in New York.

- A visit to England's sacred sites of;

  - Stonehenge

  - Glastonbury Tor
    (Climbing the Tor on Milt's 75th
    Birthday)

  - Avebury Henge

  - Chalice Well

  - Dozmary Pool
    (King Arthur's Lady of the Lake)

  - Tintagel
    (Merlin's Cave)

  - Wells Cathedral

  - Saint Michael's Tor

Guides

Susan and Milt are currently working on a proposed television series based on Susan's connection with those who inhabit the spirit world.

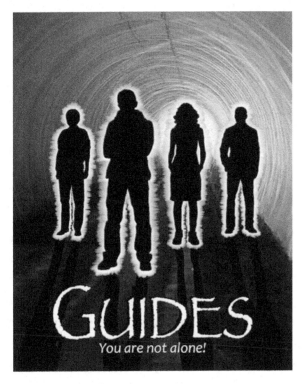

The afterlife adventures of four deceased souls who become spirit guides to help the living in their times of crisis.

To any interested Television or Movie Producers:

My name is Susan Sanderford, and I have written a pilot spec for a one-hour dramedy TV series called "Guides" that I'd like you to read. Unknown to most, we do not travel this earth-life alone! All of us have Spirit Guides to help us through our difficult times. I know this, because they have told me so. I am a spiritual medium. I communicate with Spirit Guides every day. "Guides" was written from the perspective of those now living in the spirit world, it is their story and dramatizes their world.

"Guides" is different from popular metaphysical shows such as "Medium" and "Ghost Whisperer" (shows that have proven there is a loyal audience for the paranormal genre) as "Guides" focuses on spirits helping people—rather than people helping spirits. The pilot episode, No Laughing Matter, centers on a young man named Nick, who is murdered and finds himself in a utopia-like afterlife school for Spirit Guides. There Nick is mentored by a deceased Iraq war combat soldier on how to help the living deal with their crisis situations.

Nick's first assignment is to help prevent the

suicide of a despondent stand-up comedian, Charlie Gault—an Iraq War veteran as well—who is also the estranged father of Nick's girlfriend, Abby. With the aid of a deceased, but still bitingly witty, George Carlin, Abby's quirky grandmother, and a host of other colorful Spirit Guides, Nick helps Charlie find the will to live so he can be reunited with his daughter and eventually enjoy what life has to offer.

"Guides" is a touching, yet edgy, series that will appeal to a wide audience, especially the young adult, with a love story that continues beyond death. "Guides" presents a positive, realistic, often comedic view of what is actually happening in the lives of everyday people as well as those now living in the spirit dimension.

After reading the "Guides" spec script, Broadway Pulitzer Nominated Playwright, Alexandra Gersten-Vassilaros opined—"Magical!"

Producers, drop me an email if you're interested in pursuing.

Susan Sanderford
casadesantamaria@mac.com

To learn more of Susan's spiritual mediumship abilities as well as an in-depth study of spirit communication by renowned academics in the field;

Loving Connections
(The Healing Power of After-Death Communications)

by Lisa J. Heiser, M.A., LCPC, NCC

and Jane Vair Bissler, Ph.D., LPCC, F

Available on www.amazon.com

Also Visit world famous spiritual medium James Van Praagh's website at

www.vanpraagh.com/susan-k-sanderford-2

To connect with Susan and Milt
email: casadesantamaria@mac.com

Check out YouTube videos for Mother Mary's Garden in San Luis and visit
www.casadesantamaria.org
www.susansanderford.com

To Connect with Colene Allen email:
Coleneallen@gmail.com

visit her website at
www.holisticalternativesolutions.com

If you feel led to help support Susan and Milt's effort to create this oasis of healing in the San Luis Valley in Colorado, contact them at
casadesantamaria@mac.com
Much help is needed to complete this healing oasis in Colorado's mystical San Luis Valley.

Love and love,
Susan and Milt Sanderford

Casa de Santa Maria
Make A Positive Contribution to This World!

BECOME A PART OF SOMETHING POSITIVE!

Sign up for the Casa's free monthly newsletter at
www.casadesantamaria.org

Made in the USA
Monee, IL
27 April 2021